Dionysia
Kym Deyn

VERVE
POETRY PRESS
BIRMINGHAM

PUBLISHED BY VERVE POETRY PRESS
https://vervepoetrypress.com
mail@vervepoetrypress.com

All rights reserved
© 2023 Kym Deyn

The right of Kym Deyn to be identified as author of this work has been asserted in accordance with section 77 of the Copyright, Designs and Patents Act 1988.

No part of this work may be reproduced, stored or transmitted in any form or by any means, graphic, electronic, recorded or mechanical, without the prior written permission of the publisher.

FIRST PUBLISHED SEP 2023

Printed and bound in the UK
by Imprint Digital, Exeter

ISBN: 978-1-913917-42-5

CONTENTS

Alexandros, or, the first play, consisting of

Prologue	6
Thessalonike	7
Horoscope for July 356BC	8
Note on the Nature of Thessalonike's Immortality	9
Big Fish Story	10
The Historian	11
Al-Iskander	12
Is Alexander the King Alive?	13
Thessalonike's Lament	14
Epilogue	15

Night Interludes, the second play, consisting of

The Magician	18
The Sun	20
The Lovers	22
Knight of Swords	24
The Chariot	25
The Fool	26
The High Priestess	27

Acknowledgements

For Prerana, my Achilles

'Dionysia is addictive and thrilling and perfectly formed- though you'll end up wanting more stories being re-mythed, re-mixed and re-miffed in Deyn's snappy, sharp, lyrical, ironical voice. She might indeed be Homer or Cassandra or what could happen if Greta Gerwig turned her filmic gaze to Greek myth. This is a glimmering glimpse of what one of our most compelling new writers can do.' **Kate Fox**

'In which Alexander is shown to be less than great, and Odysseus not to be trusted with the tarot cards. Kym Deyn's playful playets give these age-old myths enough topspin to make them thrum with a witty, inventive energy.' **Rishi Dastidar**

Alexandros, or

Dramatis Personae

ALEXANDER - prettyboy, wine-drunk, divine. His father's son
[whoever that is].

THESSALONIKE - the mermaid with very, very sharp teeth.
Her grief, pure as a mirror.

CALLISTHENES - nephew of Aristotle, court historian,
I'm sure he's just fine!!

FATHERS (PLURAL) - Freud is going to have something
to say about this.

MOTHER - when Alexander conquered the world
his last (unfinished) desire was to see Olympia again.

HEPHAESTION - the only thing that ever conquered Alexander
[other than wine / temper / his 33rd year]

Alexandros, or

The Death of the Historian / Mythmaking for Dummies / [fragment incomplete] / I put the sister in this because I want the impossible because grief makes madwomen of us because once she arrived she wouldn't leave and swims in this poem like a goldfish in a bowl / here she is now / scaled to her belly / soft webby hands / through alcoholic Greek waters swims / his sister.

1. Thessalonike

" Ζει ο βασιλιάς Αλέξανδρος;"
" Ζει και βασιλεύει, και τον κόσμο κυριεύει!"

CHORUS:

If we tell her the truth she'll split us clean in two
if she catches us with our lying faces on—best not
to think of it. Instead let's tell her a story:
he lives reigns conquers fucks whatever
paints his eyebrows on in the morning,
drinks coffee with the Sultan, lies drunk
in the gutter.

A man like that dead? Not likely, sister! He stepped
out for a cigarette. He'd write, but the ink runs
in seawater like blood. He's busy, Alexandria
via Teesside via The Kingdom of Heaven,
lunch with a giant spider and the Queen
of the Amazons. Besides, stamps are expensive.

He has to miss you, irreplaceable sister. Another
child can be made, another wife or lover procured.
He'll never have another Thessalonike. Not
with your shark's smile, your faint whiff of kippers.
Of course, no brother of yours could ever grow back.
Was it you? Who told him how to do it?

Myth-sister, seamaid,
               When did Alexander learn the trick?
               When was death undone?

2. Horoscope for July 356BC

This month is exceptionally auspicious for the birth
of conquerors, tyrants, manlets, sons of horned snakes,
& friends of Dorothy. [He'll look nothing like his father.]
Odd-eyed like David Bowie, maybe
he's Napoleon or Meryl Streep, any bourgeois thing.

>Today, Cancer, as everyday, beware
>of your father. Which one is up to you.
>It is a great day to change the entire
>course of history forever.

3. Note on The Nature of Thessalonike's Immortality

He could have drank the water of life,
but he washed his sister's hair in it.
If you believe the legend their blood
doesn't touch. If you believe the legend
the water was lost and Thessalonike's
red guilt doesn't reach this far
but you can't unmake an angry woman,
                imagine unsinking a ship.

4. Big Fish Story

CHORUS:
Let's recap: he survives for days inside a bell,
uses a cat as an air purifier, a chicken
to tell the time. The fish are thiiiis big,
he's taken to the impossible lands
where men have eyes in their chests,
wander about with their heads unscrewed.
Ask him, if you can, how he returned?
Ask where Faeryland leads.

You know he's in the Talmud? The story
of King Solomon's throne, the gryphons
lifting him to heaven. God waggling
his fingers, saying he's Not The Messiah. He's a very naughty—

5. The Historian

CHORUS:
Who stoppers truth? Unspins a yarn?
Arranges the inquest? Which of us draws
history's first chalk outline? For God's sake, Callisthenes!

CALLISTHENES:
(says nothing, he's very clearly dead)

CHORUS:
Attaboy! Give us something to work with. Fact's a thin morsel,
we've got a story to fanfare. What's that? Alexander's gone native?
Demanding prayer, wearing comfortable clothes? Some evenings
he forgets to be mortal at all—Locks you up,
throws away the key.

THESSALONIKE:
He didn't do it, he wasn't there! Βάλλ' εἰς κόρακας!
Bastards, hell will have you!

CHORUS:
If we had our way she wouldn't be in this bit.
But where history fails, myth grows. We can fork
our tongues. Announce the man is [not] to blame

6. Al-Iskander

the story is a wild geranium / moving this way and that / imagine a man / the rightful heir / a philosopher / wherever he goes / birds bend to omen / cities open their gates / he goes in disguise / he's a convert to whatever is sold / Pagan snakes / Jewish laws / in Ethiopia he speaks to God / he's king / conqueror / image / alchemist / his blood is ink / his being is this faint halo of light / we can say he went looking for ancestors at Achilles' shrine / we can say the treasures of Persia turned to ash with his lover's body / that he never saw his mother's face again / except in dreams / in the terrible night / of the world's edge / with God peering down / through strange white birds

7. Is Alexander the King Alive?

CHORUS:
Imagine drowning a man in it—all that gold.
His lungs a refraction of light, his golden face
preserved. It is said they put Alexander
in a vat of honey and he's in the sand somewhere
growing sweeter all the time.

THESSALONIKE:
His tomb is clean, like a god's.
He does not lie dead anywhere.

CHORUS:
There are barnacles over her ears. The omens
said he was a goner but Fishlegs is in denial.

THESSALONIKE:
Show me a body and I will show you my grief!

THESSALONIKE grabs the CHORUS by the throat

8. Thessalonike's Lament

Bitch, unsister me. When a wave rises in fury and froth and falls, that's me. Every single one is me. I'll bite you. The story returns him only in the instant of its telling. There's no one left for me to sister. I want to be a pearl unmade. All my glimmering sucked to sand. Put me in a fishtank. I'll do tricks and maul the seal trainers and ask if anyone could please tell me where my fucking brother is. Maybe I'd be better stuffed like a prize catch. You could tell everyone how I thrashed and bled how I begged at the end. I'm forever. I could watch you from a jar of formaldehyde. I don't even own this grief—it's every drop of salt. Tell me that he loves me. That the land meets the sea like a kiss. That it is not being washed away.

Alexandros, or

You might call him Alexander / boy wonder / Sekander / Al / a boy you should have known / a man you would have hated / make him parable / gay icon / monster / he's still missing out there somewhere / still asking prophets for the date of his death until he vanishes into the telling / just remember / if you ever see a seaweed girl / head bobbing in the waves / teeth glinting / you can part your lips / tell her about the man who was / Thessalonike's brother

Night Interludes

Dramatis Personae

THE FORTUNE TELLER - our narrator.

ODYSSEUS - wily Greek fox, King of Ithaca, soldier in the Trojan War.

DIOMEDES - another of Athena's favourites, soldier in the Trojan War, Odysseus' particular friend.

PENELOPE - a very clever woman. Odysseus' wife.

0. The Magician

I have done this before, Odysseus thinks, as he's invited in. How is it that every university house is a Victorian terrace in disrepair? And that everyone has bought the same vodka but no mixers and someone always breaks a gla—*Ah.*

He sits down next to someone reading Tarot cards and without looking up, they say, "You've done this before." *Last week.* "No," they say. "All of this." *Can you read my future?* "The cards are the Bible of the Carthaginians. Inherent in them is every story told and every story yet to be told." *How is it done?* "You look into the cards and see them reflect like a glass fish bowl." They shuffle. *My future?*

"The past. You were here last week."

They have not placed down a card, but are shuffling round and round. *So I was.* "With your head in a girl's lap and a boy curled up beside you." *Probably.* "And you were high." *Almost certainly.*

And in that moment of being high and being curled around the two people you love most in the world you spoke to them, asking if you thought they might have lived before.

Penelope—*her name is not Penelope*—it is.

Said that she does not think so, because she doesn't trust anything she can't see for herself. And Diomedes—*he's not Diomedes*—says that it doesn't fucking matter anyway does it. And you, Odysseus, look at them both and say you know that you have.
I did not, Odysseus says, *I fell asleep.*

But in this version of the story, you sat up on your elbows and said

[...]

1. The Sun

You'd put yourself as the centre of the story, of course, because you've never told a lie that didn't make you look good, and you've never told the truth where it painted you badly.

But truly, it begins with a man who looks like: on evenings in June in small industrial towns where the smoke spits dust into the eyes of the setting sun and it pools red light into every room of the house and the chemical stacks burn off the excess in red fire on the horizon and a sky that's never spoken before looks at its reflection and thinks red, red, red.

He's only a waiter.

But doesn't he wear his godhead well?

He comes when I call.

You smug bastard. Doesn't everyone?

The gods change like the wind and they were coming up against us. Everywhere unburied dead. Try sleeping like that, with the night and her stars stood over you. All of us seeing everyone in our dreams, living and dead and dead and dead.

And Diomedes?

They want to send someone out beyond the camp and into Trojan soil. He volunteers immediately, grinning like a lion. I look at him and think he's that moment when someone catches your eye, shot through with blue mischief, and you say "fuck off mate" and laugh but what you really mean is "I'd follow you anywhere, anywhere at all."

Diomedes is on about taking someone with him.

2. The Lovers

He said, "How could I forget my favourite schemer? Together we're like nothing else. We could pass through fire. Have you seen his mind, glimmering like a jewel?"

Was he always that nice to you?

When he wanted something.

I hadn't meant for it to happen. Sometimes people are too much even for me and then it becomes impossible to let them go.

I have an anecdote to help you demonstrate:

One night, lying in your marriage bed, Penelope turned to you and asked, "Could you really kill someone? In cold blood?"
"Of course,"
"Even me?"
"I would never,"
"But supposing. How would you do it?"
"Darling—"
"Just for curiosity's sake," she leaned over. "You won't frighten me with it."
"I'd take you by the throat and string you up from the rafters."
"Hang me? Just like that?"
"Hm. I couldn't stand to see the blood."
"Here's how I'd do it," she said.
"Kill me?" you laughed.

She whispered it to you and you turned the colour of blanched almonds.

Yes. It's just like that.

3. Knight of Swords

It's a good joke to be in on.

What?

Thinking "when this is all over, I'm going to slit your throat". Makes me smile.

Monster.

It's Diomedes who takes the spy's head off his shoulders. We race like children across the plain to the Thracians. He's laughing. A silent huff of warm air just behind my shoulder. There's a heron calling in the bushes after us.

"He really thought he could bribe his way out," I said.
Everyone thinks they can escape death, but it's winging its way closer all the time," he replied.

The Thracians have just arrived, and sleep unguarded with their weapons around them. Some deaths are closer than others, I think.

What's it like, to have the favour of the gods?

You run and don't ever have to stop. You blow out your birthday candles and the faux-retro polaroid comes out perfectly. You let a white feather go in the wind and it turns higher and higher until you can't even see it. You jump into his arms and know he's going to catch you and spin you round. You come home late and your wife's curled up on the porch swing reading a novel.

4. The Chariot

Is this what you want? The blood death? The moment a man ceases, his tongue caught between his teeth?

                                                            I'm just reporting back.

Then take the fox to the henhouse, the lurcher to the hare. The dissolution of the spirit is the same, a black wind down to hell. Ten years has made masters of us. Eyes flickering to meet in the dark and nothing at all needs to be said. We simply are. The body automata.

                      Is that what we're supposed to revere about our heroes?
                                    The tragic and the animal?

If it's making you sick then stop. All stories are wet clay, all of us are bodies snapping to attention at the sound of our names.

                                                                  I don't know how.

If the muse doesn't come, then lie. If the muse arrives let her spirit ring you round. And speak.

You kill them. Sleeping men. Their king whom they loved.

                                                    (And then we stole the horses.)

5. The Fool

Have you ever licked someone else's blood off a man's skin? Still wet and dripping off him like honey? It's almost sweet.

I watch his rolling gait in the swell. The moon patterns the sea like crushed silk. The evening air. Ripe plums. Ostensibly, we're supposed to be bathing. But I go and tug him under, waves crashing over our heads.

Later, the treasures will have sunk, the cinnabar, the ambergris, jars of sweet wine. The sea will hold you down and you will think of this. Later the sea will look like a curtain tumbling in the wind and keep you still and you will think of this.

I never see him again, do I?

Sorry.

What about—

I've already turned over the last card.

6. The High Priestess

Music thrums through the Victorian house, the cheap laminate flooring, and him. Odysseus drags his tongue over his lips.

"I had a dream about you once," the Tarot card reader confesses. "You walked out of the underworld and into this place of too much. ὦ ἱέρεια δειλιῶ. No English. I lead you through underpasses and main roads and byways covered in graffiti. The edge of the world is not measured in distance, but method." The dead speak through me in my voice.

Odysseus considers. *Who are you?*

What is there left to do,

but pretend?

"The truth of the matter is this: I'm Homer if you believe me, and Cassandra if you don't."

A NOTE ON THE GREEK:

"Ζει ο βασιλιάς Αλέξανδρος;"

"Ζει και βασιλεύει, και τον κόσμο κυριεύει!" - "Is Alexander the King alive?" This question is posed to sailors by Thessalonike, Alexander's grief-stricken sister who, in one version of the myth, throws herself in the sea after hearing of his death, where she becomes an immortal mermaid. Answering "He lives and reigns and conquers the world!" would be the only way to avoid Thessalonike's deadly wrath.

Βάλλ' εἰς κόρακας! - Literally "Go to the crows!", i.e., "go and die!"

ὦ ἱέρεια δειλιῶ - Oh priestess, I'm afraid.

ACKNOWLEDGEMENTS

With love and thanks to Fahad Al-Amoudi, Prerana Kumar, Chloe Elliot, Jay Hulme and the rest of the Durham Slamily, as well as the Writing Squad, especially Steve Dearden and Stevie Ronnie. I must also thank the Durham University Classics Department, who inspired these poems—especially Dr. Edmund Richardson, as well as my fellow students Tom Jacobs and Shannon Moxley, who made a strange and difficult time much better. Thank you to Jordon, Woody, Katherine and Signe for putting up with my tricks and accidentally helping me name this pamphlet. Thank you to Ian, my A-Level Classical Civilisations teacher, for inspiring a love of the classics that has never left, and to my parents for never stopping me from making intensely impractical choices.

ABOUT THE AUTHOR

Kym Deyn is a writer, facilitator and fortune teller based in Newcastle. They write poetry and speculative fiction and run The Braag CIC, a press and journal. Their work has been published by Broken Sleep Books, Nine Arches, Carcanet, Strange Horizons and many others. They also have a collaborative speculative fiction chapbook, Unfurl, which was written alongside Nathaniel Spain and Finlay Worrallo. Like everyone else, they are currently writing a novel. Their website is kymdeyn.com

ABOUT VERVE POETRY PRESS

Verve Poetry Press is an award-winning press that focussed initially on meeting a local need in Birmingham - a need for the vibrant poetry scene here in Brum to find a way to present itself to the poetry world via publication. Co-founded by Stuart Bartholomew and Amerah Saleh, it now publishes poets from all corners of the UK and beyond - poets that speak to the city's varied and energetic qualities and will contribute to its many poetic stories.

Added to this is a colourful pamphlet series, many featuring poets who have performed at our sister festival - and a poetry show series which captures the magic of longer poetry performance pieces by festival alumni such as Polarbear, Matt Abbott and Imogen Stirling.

The press has been voted Most Innovative Publisher at the Saboteur Awards, and has won the Publisher's Award for Poetry Pamphlets at the Michael Marks Awards.

Like the festival, we strive to think about poetry in inclusive ways and embrace the multiplicity of approaches towards this glorious art.

https://vervepoetrypress.com
@VervePoetryPres
mail@vervepoetrypress.com